EDGE
BOOKS™

U.S. ARMY
TRUE
STORIES

TALES OF BRAVERY

BY STEVEN OTFINOSKI

CAPSTONE PRESS
a capstone imprint

Edge Books are published by Capstone Press,
1710 Roe Crest Drive, North Mankato, Minnesota 56003
www.capstonepub.com

Library of Congress Cataloging-in-Publication Data
Otfinoski, Steven.
  U.S. Army true stories : tales of bravery / by Steven Otfinoski.
     pages cm—(Edge books. Courage under fire)
  Includes bibliographical references and index.
  Summary: "Provides gripping accounts of Army servicemen and servicewomen who showed
exceptional courage during combat"—Provided by publisher.
  Audience: Ages 8-12.
  ISBN 978-1-4765-9938-0 (library binding)
  ISBN 978-1-4765-9943-4 (eBook PDF)
1. United States. Army—Juvenile literature. 2. Soldiers—United States—Juvenile literature.
3. Courage—Juvenile literature. I. Title.
  UA25.O35 2015
  355.0092′273—dc23   2014004190

Editorial Credits
Christopher L. Harbo, editor; Veronica Scott, designer; Gene Bentdahl, production specialist

Photo Credits
AP Photo: John Moore, 27, 28; Corbis: Bettmann, 12, 15; iStockphotos: lauradyoung, 5 (SS);
NARA: U.S. Army Air Forces photo, 17, U.S. Army photo/Lt. Adrian C. Duff, 13; Newscom:
Everett Collection, 7, 20; Shutterstock: Gary Blakeley, 11, Gavran333, 12 (tank), Jim Barber, 5
(DSC), nazlisart, 7 (flag), 9 (flag), R Carner, 5 (BS, PH), Susan Law Cain, 10; U.S. Army photo,
23, 26, Private First Class Brandon R. Aird, cover (inset), Staff Sgt. Adelita Mead, cover, 3;
Wikimedia: Claire H., 9, NARA/James K. F. Dung, SFC, 22, NARA/U.S. Army Signal Corps
Collection, 16, public domain, 8, U. S. National Guard/Rick Reeves, 6, U.S. Coast Guard/
CPHOM Robert F. Sargent, 19, U.S.Army/Spc. Micah E. Clare, 24, 25, DoD photo, 5, 13, 21(MOH)

Design Elements
Shutterstock: Filipchuk Oleg Vasiliovich, locote, Oleg Zabielin, Petr Vaclavek

Direct Quotations
Page 8, from "Sergeant William H. Carney" by Jane Waters, New Bedford Historical
     Society (www.nbhistoricalsociety.org/sgtcarney.html).
Page 9, from "Richard Kirkland, 'The Humane Hero of Fredericksburg'" by General
     J. B. Kershaw (www.civilwar.org/education/history/primarysources/
     richard-kirkland.html).
Page 11, from *The Diary of Alvin York* by Alvin C. York (http://acacia.pair.com/Acacia.Vignettes/
     The.Diary.of.Alvin.York.html).
Page 17, from *The Permanent Book of The 20th Century: Eye-Witness Accounts of the
     Moments that Shaped Our Century* edited by Jon E. Lewis (New York: Carroll & Graf, 1994).
Page 21, from the Congressional Medal of Honor Society (www.cmohs.org/recipient-
     detail/3173/pililaau-herbert-k.php).
Page 25, from "Face of Defense: Woman Soldier Receives Silver Star" by Micah E.
     Clare, U.S. Department of Defense (www.defense.gov/news/newsarticle.aspx?id=49348).
Page 29, from "Capt. Carter's War: Test of Courage, Decency" by Chris Tomlinson,
     Los Angeles Times (http://articles.latimes.com/2003/apr/27/news/adfg-captcarter27).

Printed in the United States of America in Stevens Point, Wisconsin
032014   008092WZF14

THIS WE'LL DEFEND

The Army is the heart and soul of the United States' military. As the largest branch of the military, it has more than 500,000 soldiers ready for action. Army soldiers take the fight to enemies on the ground. They also guard and protect U.S. bases and installations around the world.

The Army also is the oldest branch of the U.S. military. It was founded on June 14, 1775, by the Second **Continental Congress**. The branch's name at that time was the Continental Army. Led by George Washington, the Army won America's independence from Great Britain during the Revolutionary War (1775–1783). Since then the Army has fought in every war the United States has entered.

While the Army's weapons and technology have changed over time, the courage of its soldiers has stayed the same. The Army's **motto** is "This We'll Defend." Army soldiers have bravely defended the United States for more than 200 years.

In the battlefront stories that follow, the brave actions of extraordinary heroes come to life. From the Civil War (1861–1865) to Operation Iraqi Freedom (2003–2011), experience the heroism of Army soldiers who displayed exceptional courage under fire.

MILITARY AWARDS

Medal of Honor:
the highest award for bravery
in the U.S. military

Distinguished Service Cross:
the second-highest military award
for bravery that is given to members
of the U.S. Army (and Air Force
prior to 1960)

Silver Star:
the third-highest award for
bravery in the U.S. military

Bronze Star:
the fourth-highest award for
bravery in the U.S. military

Purple Heart:
an award given to members
of the military wounded by
the enemy in combat

Continental Congress—leaders from the 13 original American Colonies
who served as the American government from 1774 to 1789

motto—a short statement that tells what a person or organization
believes in or stands for

THE CIVIL WAR

Dates: 1861–1865

The Combatants: Union (Northern states) vs. Confederate States of America (Southern states)

The Victor: Union

Casualties: Union—364,511 dead; Confederate—164,821 dead

Sergeant William Carney holds the flag high as the 54th Massachusetts Colored Infantry attacks Fort Wagner.

SERGEANT WILLIAM CARNEY

During the Civil War, Sergeant William Carney served in the Union's 54th Massachusetts Colored Infantry. The 54th was the first African-American **regiment** sent into battle. The regiment's very first taste of action came at James Island, South Carolina, on July 16, 1863. Two days later the regiment's soldiers arrived on Morris Island in Charleston Harbor. The 54th volunteered to lead the charge on the Confederate's heavily defended Fort Wagner.

During the attack Carney and his fellow soldiers rushed uphill to the fort. John Wall, the color sergeant, ran beside him carrying the Union flag. When Wall got hit by a bullet, Carney immediately dropped his gun. He grabbed the flag from the dying soldier and dashed toward the fort.

regiment—a large group of soldiers who fight together as a unit

Bullets whizzed by him. Two bullets struck his leg and one hit his right arm. Badly wounded, he finally reached the fort's wall and planted the flag in the sand.

Unable to take the fort, Union forces retreated. But Carney refused to leave the flag behind. Other soldiers tried to take the flag from him as they helped him to safety, but he wouldn't let it go. Stumbling and crawling,

Carney with the flag he saved

he finally made it back to the Union ranks. When he arrived he told his regiment, "The old Flag never touched the ground."

Nearly half of the 54th's 600 soldiers died in the attack on Fort Wagner. Many years after the war, Carney was honored for his bravery. He earned the Medal of Honor. He was the first African-American to receive the honor.

SERGEANT RICHARD KIRKLAND

The Angel of Mayre's Heights statue

On December 13, 1862, the Civil War's Battle of Fredericksburg entered its third day. Union forces charged across a field at Mayre's Heights in Virginia. Meanwhile, Confederate troops awaited them behind a long stone wall. The Confederates mowed down wave after wave of Union soldiers. By dawn on December 14, hundreds of wounded Union soldiers cried out for help. Confederate sergeant Richard Kirkland asked Brigadier General Joseph Kershaw if he could take them water. Kershaw refused, but Kirkland kept asking.

The general finally let him go. Kirkland filled every canteen he could find with water. Then he crawled over the wall and crept toward the wounded soldiers. Union sharpshooters thought Kirkland was stealing from dead soldiers. They fired on him. But they stopped when they realized he had come to help. General Kershaw later wrote: "For an hour and a half did this ministering angel pursue his labor of mercy ... until he had relieved all of the wounded on that part of the field." Today a statue of "The Angel of Mayre's Heights" stands near the wall Kirkland bravely crossed.

WORLD WAR I

Dates: 1914–1918

The Combatants: Allies (main countries: Great Britain, France, Italy, Russia, United States) vs. Central Powers (main countries: Germany, Austria-Hungary, Bulgaria, Ottoman Empire)

The Victor: Allies

Casualties: Allies–5,142,631 dead; Central Powers–3,386,200 dead

American soldiers in the trenches of France during World War I

SERGEANT ALVIN YORK

Sergeant Alvin York was born on a farm in the mountains of Tennessee. When the United States entered World War I in 1917, York refused to join the Army. His religion was against war. But the U.S. government did not recognize his church. York was **drafted** and reluctantly went off to fight in France.

On October 8, 1918, York and a group of 16 American soldiers set out to capture a railroad in France's Argonne Forest. German machine gun teams spotted the Americans as they were coming around a hill and opened fire. Nine soldiers on the right **flank** were killed or wounded. York was hidden from view on the left flank. He started firing back. He later described what happened next. "I was right out in the open and the machine guns were spitting fire and cutting up all around me something awful. But they didn't seem to be able to hit me." York's rifle grew hot in his hands. His ammunition was almost gone, but he kept firing. By the time the smoke cleared, nine German machine gunners lay dead. York's courage inspired his remaining comrades. They took out 25 more Germans.

draft—to select young men to serve in the military
flank—the right or left of a military formation

The German commander thought he was up against a large American force and surrendered. York and the remaining American soldiers captured 132 German soldiers. He and his men marched their prisoners 10 miles (16 kilometers) to the American headquarters in Varennes. York returned home a hero and received the Medal of Honor for his actions.

Sergeant Alvin York

CORPORAL DONALD CALL

Donald Call was a stage actor before World War I. However, no role he played was more dramatic than the one he filled on the battlefield near Varennes, France.

On September 26, 1918, Call and an officer were using their tank to fight German machine gun nests. Suddenly an **artillery** shell blew half the tank's **turret** off. Gas filled the tank, making it difficult to breathe. Call scrambled out of the tank and ran for safety.

American tank in World War I

But when Call turned around, the officer wasn't behind him. Without a second thought, Call dashed back to the tank. Dodging enemy gunfire and falling shells, he climbed back into the tank. He found the officer alive but unable to move. He pulled him from the tank. Then he carried him 1 mile (1.6 km) through the battlefield while **snipers** fired at them. After the war Call received the Medal of Honor for his courage.

---

artillery—cannons and other large guns used during battles
turret—a rotating, armored structure that holds a weapon on top of a vehicle
sniper—a soldier trained to shoot at long-distance targets from a hidden place

PRIVATE HENRY JOHNSON

Private Henry Johnson served in France during World War I. One night while he was on guard duty, the Germans attacked. Sniper bullets whizzed by Johnson and Private Needham Roberts. Suddenly the "snip-snip" sound of someone cutting through the protective fence floated out of the darkness. Johnson realized the Germans were closing in. He sent Roberts back to warn their camp. But a German grenade wounded Roberts' hip and arm. Roberts crawled back to Johnson for safety.

Johnson told Roberts to stay down and hand him grenades. He hurled every grenade they had, but the Germans kept coming. Johnson was shot in the head and lip, but he fired his rifle until it jammed. More bullets pierced his body. Johnson swung his rifle like a club at the advancing Germans. When they knocked him down, he jumped up with his knife in hand. He stabbed at Germans trying to take Roberts prisoner. Finally, French and American soldiers arrived and forced the Germans to retreat. Johnson passed out and was taken to a field hospital. Doctors discovered 21 wounds on his body. The next day, soldiers learned Johnson had taken out four Germans and wounded 10 others.

private—a soldier of the lowest rank

Private Henry Johnson's hand-to-hand combat with the Germans earned him the nickname "Black Death" during World War I.

Both Johnson and Roberts survived the attack. For their courage, they became the first American privates to be awarded the Croix du Guerre. It is France's highest military honor. For his fighting skills, Henry Johnson earned the nickname "Black Death."

WORLD WAR II

DATES: 1939–1945

THE COMBATANTS: ALLIES (MAIN COUNTRIES: GREAT BRITAIN, FRANCE, RUSSIA, UNITED STATES) VS. AXIS POWERS (MAIN COUNTRIES: GERMANY, ITALY, JAPAN)

THE VICTOR: ALLIES

CASUALTIES: ALLIES—14,141,544 DEAD; AXIS—5,634,232 DEAD

American troops approach Omaha Beach on a landing craft during the D-Day invasion on June 6, 1944.

CAPTAIN JOSEPH DAWSON

June 6, 1944, was the turning point of World War II. Thousands of American soldiers landed on the beaches along France's Normandy coast during the D-Day invasion. Their goal was to take the country back from the Germans. Many heroes stormed the beaches that day. One of them was Captain Joseph Dawson.

When Dawson and his 1st Infantry Division landed on Omaha Beach, German gunners awaited them. The Germans rained down firepower. Bullets cut the air around Dawson and his men. But he charged ahead, scrambling up the beach with his men in tow. Along the way, Dawson was shot in the knee and right leg. Still, he pressed forward. As they approached the crest of a hill, Dawson heard German voices. "I could now hear the Germans talking in the machine gun nest immediately above me," he later explained. Despite his wounds, Dawson tossed two grenades into the nest. The blasts silenced the machine gun fire.

By the end of the day, Dawson and his men had gone farther inland than any other American soldiers. For his bravery and leadership that day, Dawson received the Distinguished Service Cross.

But Dawson's bravery during the war didn't end on Omaha Beach. As the Americans pushed through France toward Paris, Dawson continued to fight. He rescued an American **platoon** ambushed by enemies.

Later in 1944 Dawson's company seized a ridge overlooking the German city of Aachen. Wave after wave of German soldiers attacked the ridge. But Dawson and his men refused to give up. They defended the ridge for 39 days. Their courage allowed other American troops to take Aachen. It was the first German city to fall to the Allies in the war. The ridge was later named "Dawson's Ridge" in his honor.

platoon—a small group of soldiers who work together

The U.S. Army's 1st Division slogs through the water before storming Omaha Beach.

THE KOREAN WAR

DATES: 1950–1953

THE COMBATANTS: THE UNITED STATES, SOUTH KOREA, AND UNITED NATIONS (UN) TROOPS VS. NORTH KOREA AND CHINA

THE VICTOR: NO VICTOR; THE UN AND NORTH KOREA SIGNED A TRUCE, BUT NO PERMANENT PEACE TREATY WAS EVER SIGNED BY NORTH KOREA AND SOUTH KOREA

CASUALTIES: UNITED STATES, UN, AND SOUTH KOREA–256,631 DEAD; CHINESE AND NORTH KOREANS–ESTIMATED 1,006,000 DEAD

American soldiers hunker down in trenches during the Korean War.

PRIVATE HERBERT PILILAAU

Herbert Pililaau was a gentle soul from Hawaii. He was also a fine singer who played the ukulele. But while serving his country in the Korean War, he fought fiercely to protect his fellow soldiers.

Private Pililaau served in a platoon stationed on "Heartbreak Ridge" near Pia-ri, Korea. On September 17, 1951, a huge wave of North Korean soldiers tried to take the ridge from the Americans. Pililaau and his platoon fought off the enemy until they were almost out of ammunition. Officers ordered the men to move to a safer location. Pililaau volunteered to stay behind to provide cover fire for the retreating soldiers. When his gun ran out of bullets, Pililaau began lobbing grenades at the enemy. When the grenades ran out, he pulled out his knife. He fought the attackers in hand-to-hand combat. He finally swung at them with his fists until they overwhelmed him.

Later Pililaau's platoon members retook the area and recovered his body. The bodies of more than 40 enemy soldiers surrounded him. Pililaau is believed to have killed most—if not all—of them himself.

Pililaau received the Medal of Honor **posthumously**. It was given for "conspicuous [outstanding] gallantry [bravery] … at the risk of his life above and beyond the call of duty."

posthumous—coming or happening after death

THE VIETNAM WAR

DATES: 1959–1975

THE COMBATANTS: UNITED STATES, SOUTH VIETNAM, AND THEIR ALLIES VS. NORTH VIETNAM AND ITS ALLIES

THE VICTOR: NORTH VIETNAM

CASUALTIES: UNITED STATES–58,220 DEAD; SOUTH VIETNAM–ESTIMATED 200,000 TO 250,000 DEAD; NORTH VIETNAM–ESTIMATED 1.1 MILLION DEAD

U.S. Army helicopters pick up soldiers after a mission in South Vietnam.

SERGEANT BILLY WALKABOUT

Helping wounded soldiers while being seriously injured is the mark of a true hero. On November 20, 1968, Sergeant Billy Walkabout, who was a Cherokee Indian, and 12 other soldiers came under heavy fire behind enemy lines. One man was seriously wounded. Walkabout gave the man first aid and radioed for a helicopter.

While loading the injured soldier onto the chopper, a land mine blew up. The blast killed three men. The rest, including Walkabout, were wounded. But Walkabout still rushed from man to man, treating their wounds.

As more helicopters landed, Walkabout helped load the wounded into them. He refused to be taken to safety until all of his fellow soldiers were safely aboard the choppers.

Walkabout's heroism earned him a Distinguished Service Cross. In addition he earned a Purple Heart, five Silver Stars, and five Bronze Stars during his 23 months in Vietnam. He was one of the most decorated soldiers to serve in the war.

OPERATION ENDURING FREEDOM

DATES: 2001–PRESENT

THE COMBATANTS: AFGHANISTAN GOVERNMENT, THE UNITED STATES AND ITS COALITION FORCES VS. AL-QAIDA **TERRORIST** ORGANIZATION AND THE TALIBAN, AN ISLAMIC GROUP THAT SUPPORTS AL-QAIDA

THE VICTOR: CONFLICT ONGOING

CASUALTIES: AMERICAN AND COALITION FORCES (THROUGH DECEMBER 6, 2012)–3,215 DEAD; AFGHAN CIVILIANS (REPORTED FROM JANUARY 2007 TO JUNE 2012)–13,009 DEAD; TALIBAN AND AL-QAIDA–NUMBER UNKNOWN

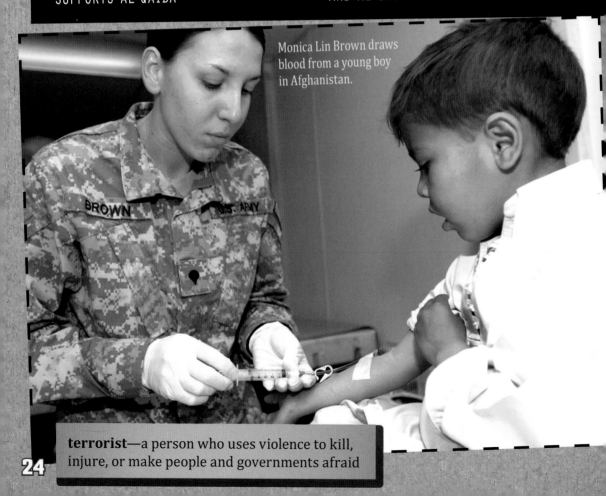

Monica Lin Brown draws blood from a young boy in Afghanistan.

terrorist—a person who uses violence to kill, injure, or make people and governments afraid

24

ARMY SPECIALIST MONICA LIN BROWN

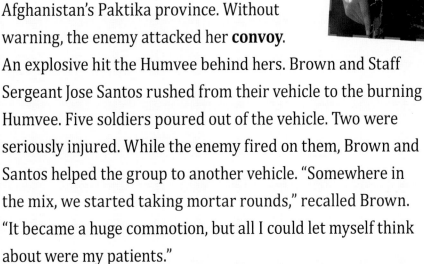

On April 25, 2007, Army medic Monica Lin Brown was on a security patrol in Afghanistan's Paktika province. Without warning, the enemy attacked her **convoy**. An explosive hit the Humvee behind hers. Brown and Staff Sergeant Jose Santos rushed from their vehicle to the burning Humvee. Five soldiers poured out of the vehicle. Two were seriously injured. While the enemy fired on them, Brown and Santos helped the group to another vehicle. "Somewhere in the mix, we started taking mortar rounds," recalled Brown. "It became a huge commotion, but all I could let myself think about were my patients."

Bullets flew everywhere as Brown prepared the men for helicopter rescue. At last the enemy retreated. Brown helped the wounded men to the arriving helicopter. Without her aid they may not have survived.

For her bravery Brown received a Silver Star. She was only the second woman since World War II to receive this honor.

convoy—group of vehicles traveling together, usually accompanied by armed forces

STAFF SERGEANT CLINTON ROMESHA

Staff Sergeant Clinton Romesha was stationed at a remote valley outpost in Afghanistan's Nuristan province. On October 3, 2009, 300 Taliban fighters attacked the outpost with machine guns and rocket grenades.

Romesha returned fire. He shot one machine gun team with a sniper's rifle. Then a rocket grenade struck the electric generator he was hiding behind. **Shrapnel** wounded his neck, shoulder, and arms, but he kept fighting. He gathered a team of five men, and they counterattacked. Romesha radioed the location of the enemy to the operations center. They sent in aircraft that took out another 30 Taliban fighters.

Eight Americans were killed and 22 wounded in the fierce fighting. But thanks to Romesha, the outpost was not taken. On February 11, 2013, he was awarded the Medal of Honor.

shrapnel—pieces that have broken off something after an explosion

OPERATION IRAQI FREEDOM

DATES: 2003-2011

THE COMBATANTS: THE UNITED STATES AND COALITION FORCES VS. IRAQ, FIRST THE GOVERNMENT OF SADDAM HUSSEIN AND THEN **INSURGENTS**

THE VICTOR: THE UNITED STATES DEFEATED SADDAM HUSSEIN IN 2003 BUT THEN FACED STIFF FIGHTING FROM INSURGENTS UNTIL ITS WITHDRAWAL IN 2011

CASUALTIES: AMERICAN AND COALITION FORCES—4,804 DEAD; IRAQI SOLDIERS AND INSURGENTS—ESTIMATED MORE THAN 30,000 DEAD

Smoke billows from a burning car on a bridge controlled by Army forces in Al Hindiyah, Iraq.

insurgent—a person who rebels and fights against his or her country's ruling government and those supporting it

CAPTAIN CHRIS CARTER

On March 31, 2003, the main U.S. forces invading Iraq prepared to enter the Karbala Gap. This 1-mile- (1.6-km-) wide passage would bring troops closer to the capital city of Baghdad. But the military wanted to fool the Iraqis into thinking they were moving elsewhere. Captain Chris Carter and his company had orders to enter the city of Al Hindiyah to take control of a bridge. Carter's company carried out the **diversion** with tanks and other armed vehicles. Iraqi troops fired machine guns and hurled grenades as the troops passed.

Captain Chris Carter calls for an armored ambulance to come to the aid of an injured Iraqi woman on March 31, 2003.

diversion—an attack that draws the attention of the enemy away from the real point of attack

Carter held his position in front of the bridge for several hours. Then a soldier spotted an elderly Iraqi woman lying in the middle of the bridge. She had gotten caught up in the battle, and she was waving for help. Carter leaped into action. He ordered an armored vehicle to move toward the bridge while he and two other soldiers followed on foot.

When they reached the woman, Carter threw a smoke grenade so the enemy couldn't see them clearly. The captain knelt by the woman and gave her water. He discovered she was bleeding and radioed for an armored ambulance. When it arrived, the two soldiers carried the woman to safety. Carter provided cover by firing at the enemy.

Later Carter was asked why he saved the woman in the middle of fierce fighting. He said he came to Iraq to fight "... for the people. To leave her out on that bridge would have gone against the grain of why we are here."

Throughout U.S. history millions of Army soldiers have proudly defended their country. Time and again, they have risked their lives—never thinking twice about putting themselves in harm's way. Their tales show us the courage and skill of our fighting men and women in the line of fire.

artillery (ar-TI-luhr-ee)—cannons and other large guns used during battles

Continental Congress (KAHN-tuh-nen-tuhl KAHN-gruhs)—leaders from the 13 original American Colonies who served as the American government from 1774 to 1789

convoy (CON-voi)—group of vehicles traveling together, usually accompanied by armed forces

diversion (duh-VUR-zhuhn)—an attack that draws the attention of the enemy away from the real point of attack

draft (DRAFT)—to select young men to serve in the military

flank (FLANK)—the right or left of a military formation

insurgent (in-SUR-juhnt)—a person who rebels and fights against his or her country's ruling government and those supporting it

motto (MOT-oh)—a short statement that tells what a person or organization believes in or stands for

platoon (pluh-TOON)—a small group of soldiers who work together

posthumous (POHST-huh-muhss)—coming or happening after death

private (PRYE-vit)—a soldier of the lowest rank

regiment (REJ-uh-muhnt)—a large group of soldiers who fight together as a unit

shrapnel (SHRAP-nuhl)—pieces that have broken off something after an explosion

sniper (SNY-pur)—a soldier trained to shoot at long-distance targets from a hidden place

terrorist (TER-ur-ist)—a person who uses violence to kill, injure, or make people and governments afraid

turret (TUR-it)—a rotating, armored structure that holds a weapon on top of a vehicle

READ MORE

Huey, Lois Miner. *Voices of World War II: Stories from the Front Lines.* Voices of War. Mankato, Minn.: Capstone Press, 2011.

Perritano, John. *World War I.* America at War. New York: Franklin Watts, 2010.

Yomtov, Nel. *True Stories of the Civil War.* War Stories. North Mankato, Minn.: Capstone Press, 2013.

SELECT BIBLIOGRAPHY

Birdwell. Michael. "Sgt. Alvin York," WorldWar1.com, www.worldwar1.com/heritage/sgtayork.htm.

Clare, Micah E. "Face of Defense: Woman Soldier Receives Silver Star." U.S. Department of Defense, March 24, 2008, www.defense. gov/news/newsarticle.aspx?id=49348.

King, Gilbert. "Remembering Henry Johnson, the Soldier Called 'Black Death,'" Smithsonianmag.com, October 25, 2011, www. smithsonianmag.com/history/remembering-henry-johnson-the-soldier-called-black-death-117386701.

Landler, Mark. "Obama Awards Medal of Honor to Clinton Romesha," *New York Times*, February 11, 2013, www.nytimes. com/2013/02/12/us/politics/obama-awards-medal-of-honor-to-clinton-romesha.html?_r=0.

Waters, Jane. "Sergeant William H. Carney (1840–1908)," New Bedford Historical Society, www.nbhistoricalsociety.org/sgtcarney.html.

Wyckoff, Mac. "Richard Kirland, the Angel of Marye's Heights," Fredericksburg.com, http://fredericksburg.com/CivilWar/Battle/kirkland.htm.

FactHound offers a safe, fun way to find Internet sites related to this book. All of the sites on FactHound have been researched by our staff.

Here's all you do:

Visit www.facthound.com

Type in this code: 9781476599380

 Check out projects, games and lots more at
www.capstonekids.com